DANCE AGAINST THE WALL

ALSO BY JOHN L. STANIZZI

Windows
Ecstasy Among Ghosts
Sleepwalking

DANCE AGAINST THE WALL

Poems by

John L. Stanizzi

Antrim House
Simsbury, Connecticut

Dec 2012
er Jennifer
with gratitude
Thanks for everything.

John

Library of Congress Control Number: 2012947545

ISBN: 978-1-936482-35-1

Printed & bound by United Graphics, Inc.

First Edition, 2012

Book design by Rennie McQuilkin

Front cover photograph by the author

Front cover design by Steve Straight

Author photograph by Carol Stanizzi

Antrim House
860.217.0023
AntrimHouse@comcast.net
www.AntrimHouseBooks.com
21 Goodrich Road, Simsbury, CT 06070

for my father, Giovannino Emmanuele Stanizzi

and my mother, Felicia Rose DeCorleto Stanizzi

ACKNOWLEDGMENTS

Grateful acknowledgment is made to the following publications in which these poems first appeared, some of them in earlier versions:

burntdistrict: "Confession"
Carcinogenic Poetry: "Firefly"
Chaffey Review: "Broken"
Combustus: "Adjustment," "Tattoos," "Lye"
Freshwater: "Communion," "Promises After Ellis Island"
Gutter Eloquence: " Promise"
Hawk & Handsaw: "The Dutiful Car"
Indigo Rising (UK): "Path," "Broken," "Recall," "Waiting," "Children"
InStereoPress: "The Language of Trees"
MadSwirl: " Fiction"
New York Quarterly: "Watches"
nibble: "Mow the Apples"
Passages North: "Farmer"
Penwood Review: "Tireless Neighbor"
PoetSpeak.com (audio and text): "Back Pages," "Hawk"
Puckerbrush Review: "DLROW," "In Thunder, Lightning, or in Rain?" "Voices"
Red Headed Stepchild: "Is Is"
Rhubarb (Canada): "DLROW," "Protecting Assets," "Looking For It"
Solo Novo: "Glow-in-the-dark Crucifix"
Theodate: "Treefrog"
Third Wednesday: "Mice"
Thrush: "Comet"
Tiger's Eye: "Son"
The Toucan: "High and Inside," "The Language of Trees," "Hawk"
Wild Goose Poetry Review: "Front," "Kayak," "The Hat"

Very special thanks to my father, who taught me everything, including the importance of generosity, what it means to give your word, and the rewards of working hard. Thanks also to my mother for her strength. Thanks and praises to my best friend, my wife Carol, to my amazing children and grandchildren, my family, my colleagues at Bacon Academy and Manchester Community College, and to Rennie McQuilkin for his measureless contributions to the art of poetry and for all that he has done for me.

TABLE OF CONTENTS

I. THE ROAD HOME

II. MOWING THE APPLES

Infinite emptiness will be all around you,
all the resurrected dead of all the ages
wouldn't fill it, and there you'll be like a
little bit of grit in the middle of the steppe.

Hamm in "Endgame,"
Samuel Beckett

Sometimes you just have to pee in the sink.

Charles Bukowski

Well, it is a steep mountain to climb
And it is a deep river to cross
The road is rocky and rough
So I can't afford for my soul to lost.

Capleton, "Steep Mountain"

DANCE AGAINST THE WALL

I. THE ROAD HOME

BACK PAGES

For my father

Ah, but I was so much older then,
I'm younger than that now.

    "My Back Pages," Bob Dylan

Just another day of flawless clarity,
as the gray canvas tarp of the dying river
nudged the distended carcasses of rotting fish
under a sky that no one ever noticed,
and you, the hod-carrier's middle boy,
running from the bakery to your flat,
your stolen loaves of bread still warm and soft.

            *

Frankie and Rosario out in front
every summer night for stick ball games.
Batting once, Frankie swung and missed,
rapped you hard and broke your Roman nose,
umbo on its bridge they never fixed,
aquiline distinction embarrassing you,
regardless of the jokes you always make.
You remember this with alacrity.

            *

Memories of joining the service out of spite,
and still the old man counted your army pay.
Reaching for your wallet, he'd stare at you,

condemning you for walking out on him;
his share was every penny that you earned.

*

Angelo was the first to mutiny,
packed whatever he possessed and left.
Retelling this you never forget his gun
inside the zipper pocket of an old suitcase.
Legends are made in dirty hotel rooms.

*

Men grow up to see their fathers die,
and you remember yours as strong and good,
yet years would pass before you forgave his faults.

*

Joey showed up drunk one Christmas Eve,
undid what little grace your family had;
nine guys couldn't bring him down.
Every year you resurrect that tale.

*

Jalopy parked against the curb, you posed
under the murky light that lit the sign —
Lun On Company Chinese Grocery —
you and Dolly in each other's arms.

*

And after that she brought you home to Mama.
Useless to try and hide the truth from her;
grease-ball alley cat was all you were,
underprivileged thug who came from Front
Street's slums. Her daughter certainly would not give
the time of day to a cross-town wop like you.

*

Soon enough you'd get to know her dad;
every night you'd go and find him drunk,
permanent fixture in the Red Ash Grille,
the Mayor of Albany Avenue holding court,
early evenings giving in to neon,
memories that, in spite of things forgotten,
burn as if they happened yesterday,
every one a clear and perfect scene,
reminiscence that won't abandon you.

*

Once there was a time that you would joke —
"CRS," you'd laugh to all your friends,
then entire decades began to gray.
"Old Timer's Disease? What the fuck is that?"
Behind the now of the moment we are in
each remembrance turning into dust,
reaching back to where they used to be.

*

No memories can return; they don't exist.
Oh, you will always be a business man,
veracious entrepreneur of your own making
endeavoring to work with dignity,
manual labor a constant source of pride,
but nowadays the road to work is strange,
every street some exotic foreign land,
relics of the streetlights burning out.

*

During the day now you are in your cellar
eking out a past from yellowed photos,
collages used to trap old memories,
each one carefully cut and placed and framed.
Mid-morning you will go out in your yard;
behind your stockade fence you will take off
everything except your underwear,
rattle a bell for the animals to come,

*

get down feebly on your iron knees,
offering peanuts to the squirrel you've named,
never once thinking about the days'
evanescent trek from light to dark.

THE DUTIFUL CAR

My father makes his way to his grandson's home,
with his navigator, my mother, at his side.
It's not the easiest trip, what with the snow
and ice, and these days driving in the dark
is more than he can handle; he's having trouble
in the light of day, but in the night,
which can eclipse the senses of the best,
even with the light of torrential stars,
we are asking just a little bit too much.

They arrive at the party to everyone's delight,
leaving their car by the curb in the frigid cold,
and my father wants to know whose house we're at.
It occurs to me as I struggle to find the good
that it's a bit like seeing everything for
the first time every time that you arrive.
You learn to tell yourself these private lies.

He tosses his keys in the basket on the table
and begins his quest to find a glass of wine.
Out in the street his car is idling quietly,
plumes of exhaust wafting in the cold,
the parking lights' illusion of some warmth,
the tranquil, barely audible purr of heat.
I notice this and ask him for his keys,
press the button of his automatic-start,
and check to be sure that the car is really off.

People graze around the kitchen table,
dipping chips in salsa, crunching veggies,
talking loudly over the UConn game,

while out in the street the car is running again.
I surmise that someone bumped the starter
in the basket. How else can you explain
the fact that my father's empty car is on,
warming quietly in the February night?

I press the button on the little pad,
looking out the window to be sure
the car has done what it's supposed to do,
the column of exhaust no longer there,
the orange lights no longer visible.

The guests have now begun to fix their plates,
the festive table of cheese and cold-cut platters,
tubs of salads, jars of mayonnaise,
our favorite team losing another game.

Then someone says, "The car is on again."
And sure enough there's that curl of smoke,
his car impatient on the icy street,
parking lights to guide him to its warmth,
the motor purring, the heater on just right.
And picking up the key-ring one more time,
I tell myself another private lie.

I think about the dutiful car out front
defying all the odds of technology
so when he walks into the winter night
and makes his way along the icy path,
it will be ready, eager to guide his way,
having spent the evening insistent on warmth.
In the inviting shimmer of parking lights,
he will study the maps to bring him safely home.

DLROW

The first test they give him
is to see if he can spell
world backwards,
which he can, easily—
such demeaning, useless exercises
at Yale,
Mecca of miracles
where she is sure
they'll give him a pill one day
to reverse it all
and bring him back.

But for now
no matter the day of the week,
his birth date,
the season,
the one thing he knows for sure
is that the world is backwards,
and it will be that way from now on.

LOOKING FOR IT

Then it was all dark, and his white crib
and the dim faces that moved above him,
and the warm sweet aroma of the milk
faded out altogether from his mind.

      "The Curious Case of Benjamin
      Button," F. Scott Fitzgerald

My father said

I we
were out
back there where they

what do you call it

where they

plant the

you know

boom boom
guys coming
all over the yard

then
boom!

down back there looking and looking
for it looking

it'll turn up
just gotta keep

turning

the stones over

turn 'em over

it's gonna be there

and we'll get some guys
you
and me
huh?

boom

down back there by the brook your mother
and me

she's

I don't know

was here a minute ago

just keep turning them over
looking for it

can't find the damn thing.

And I said, stupidly,

At least you're out getting some air,

and he laughed,
recognizing my patronizing ignorance
and said

So what's up?

in the old tone of voice,
that vestige of clarity,
the inspiration for

He's doing all right.

And if, in the end,
the moment is sufficient,
if it is enough
to have just the moment
only for the instant it flashes
then he *is* doing all right,
everything he ever was
vanishing into the air,
a flimsy dream floating away
from beneath turned stones.

PROTECTING ASSETS

When you could no longer sign your name,
when the only things you responded to
were the bumps in the road
and the one street sign you recognized —
when this happened,
and oh yes,
when complete sentences were things
other people did,
you became silent,
though you wouldn't call it silence;
you wouldn't call it anything…
When these things happened
it was decided,
for you,
what was best,
and what was best,
as far as you could tell,
was to sit there, mute,
while whole sentences unraveled
and the string of your signature unraveled
and street signs became blank
and the road home was dark anyway,
winding and covered with rubble.

ADJUSTMENT

My father sits in his Barcalounger,
pajama bottoms, plaid shirt, dress shoes.

I sit on the edge of his bed,

and my mother
is standing between us,
saying
"Yes, this is our son.
This is Johnnie.
Yes, you recognize him,"

and I look up from the paper
to meet his eyes for a moment,

and he makes it clear
that he has no idea who I am,
goes back to humming Mario Lanza
and playing with little plastic army men

while I look down to read that
the Knicks are on a six-game run,
a vague sense of transient contentment
there in the space between us.

ABSENCE

"When was the last time you saw your son?"
I ask my father,
sitting next to him at the table.

He wrinkles his brow,
thinks deeply.
"My son? Jesus. I haven't seen him in a long, long time."

And I think maybe he's right,
maybe I have been gone a long time,
maybe I've been gone for years.

TATTOOS

Unlike the other men in the family, my father
has no chains or skunks with attitude,
or his last name over crossed Italian flags,
no *Mom* or *Born to Ride* or broken heart,
no *Semper Fi,* no naked ladies or dice.

My father has no Jolly Rogers or devils,
no angels, crosses, lions, dragons, or knives.
He has no rosary beads or praying hands,
no Virgin with child, *U.S. Army* or dove.
My father has no Sacred Heart of Jesus.

But on the inside of his left forearm
there's one tattoo no bigger than a signature
and the same shade of faded blue as the bruises
that blossom on his papery yellow skin,
and as he sits in his big reclining chair,
smiling vaguely and squeezing a stuffed toy,
I glimpse the washed-out ink that tells the story:
Johnny and Dolly, faded and just about gone.

IN THUNDER, LIGHTNING, OR IN RAIN?

for Clem

This morning's storm brings Clem to mind
in those days before she sat
gently petting the napkin in her lap,
and whispering "kitty…kitty…"
before the perfume of the herb garden grew senseless
and old photographs faded until they were just objects
her hands turned over and over,

before her shoulders hunched
and her eyes gazed past everything here,
her face pressed against the wall
as if she could simply pass through into another room,
leaving poems and the Sunday roast,
before she left altogether, finally
drifting away into the foul heath,

but after she had forgotten what a car was,
and how to fold the memory
of her body into the front seat,
after she needed to be steered,
hands placed lightly behind each of her elbows,
her small voice whispering with vague surety
to whoever was there,
"When shall we three meet again?"
full of the knowledge that she was leaving,
surer still that she was not yet gone.

RECALL

Finally summer has come and we all wear
humidity as if it were a coat
of fabric much too thick for muggy days
in which the trees can only nod assent

that yes, it is the humidity not the heat.
And two young boys at play on a river bank
many years ago could only think
that the river water, wide and brown and swift

that carried along distended, fetid fish
and teemed with insects rising into the stench
of sluggish afternoons in mid-July
was all they needed to know of Paradise.

They could not know that swimming through that mire
was indeed a journey into dazzling light,
but that they were also carried toward a dark
as ponderous and empty as the filthy river

which dragged itself along, a tired weight;
they couldn't dream of the empty spaces ahead
through which they would emerge as older men
looking off into the sultry hills,

staring through the vacancy that was left behind
by brothers and fathers walking away from here,
leaving the men too weary to reconcile,
lifting sweaty glasses to their lips.

GLOW-IN-THE-DARK CRUCIFIX

He hung on His cross above my bed for years,
withered and wasted, a limp weight, nearly
naked, the closest I had come to seeing
an unclothed body, and so more sensuous than sacred,
The Messiah arousing something strange and addictive
and still unnamed, this green figurine
irresistibly disconcerting, His
golden locks, the terrible crown of thorns,
the agonizing blueness of his eyes...

That was a composite from my imagination,
born of the pictures hung on my aunt's yellowed wall,
all the doubt that night in Gethsemene,
praying Himself into a fear-filled sweat,
and the offering of the flaming, external heart,
pierced by every sinner in the world,
but when I took a closer look at Him,
this Saviour had a seam around himself —
to separate the Son of God from man?
He had a face like melted candlewax;
when He became the light from within the light
until the light that He became dissolved,
His no eyes looked toward the sky—at nothing.

II. Mowing the Apples

F

St. Mary's School, East Hartford, CT

Mother Superior makes me come to the front of the class,
hands me a red pen
and demands I write a big *F* on my report card,
an *F* bigger than the box provided next to *Conduct,*
which is trouble
because I know there is no lie good enough
for my parents to believe,
and I feel trapped —
so later I lick my pencil eraser
and try and try to erase the red *F,*
but all I manage is to wear a hole in my report card
where the *F* had been,
so I decide not to show them,
which is also trouble
because Mother Superior
has called home
to tell them about the red *F*
and about how bad I am,
and my mother beats me with a wooden spoon
and my father gets drunk and leaves,
all because of me
and the horrible things I have done.

CHILDREN

The children of the lake are striped and grimy,
their little bodies made from scraps of bone,
their enormous heads precarious atop
their pencil necks protruding from knobby shoulders

like yokes made from the bones of some small bird,
and as they splat around the shallow marsh,
running single file with a tentative gait,
carrying massive buckets in their tiny hands,

the leader's voice pierces the calming haze
of the sunset which only hints at the coming night
and bellows forth an affirmation that, Yes!
there is a frog sitting right next to the shore,

bring the bucket, bring the net, he's ours!
And the children of the lake proceed undaunted,
as we observe them from atop the hill.
The lawn on which we stand reaches out before us,

darkening as it slopes down toward the marsh
where we can still make out the silver boat
that leans against the blackened, iron fence,
and the blue canoe upside down beneath

the paper birch that sparkles in the yard;
and we can still make out the sticky path,
slick and wet between the lawn and marsh,
where the pond lilies' yellow deepens to a shadowy dark

and a small peninsula separates marsh and lake,
where the jagged, neon reflection of glancing light
rocks across the surface of the water;
and the far beach is foreground for the windows

of amber light that glow in perfect order,
a distant image of the comforting light we cast
against the encroaching dusk where children run
in pursuit of living things they might collect,

and we smile as if we know these tired children,
a melancholy smile of recognition.

POTATOES

Christmas, 1961

It's a bright blue night
a week after Christmas
and I'm dragging a used Christmas tree
through the woods to Gilman's Pond,
one or two remnant strands
of tinsel glinting weakly.

Someone has kindled a small fire,
and the scrape of blades on lumpy ice
rattles in the stalagtites of light
that reach down through knuckled winter branches,
and in the gray glow
there in the woods by the pond,
I empty my pockets
of the paper packets of salt and pepper
my grandmother has taken
from the Triple A Diner,
and place them
on the big log next to the fire.

Then I lay the Christmas tree across the small flames;
there is a pause,
a silence for the moment
it takes the flames to find the dry needles,
and then the detonation,
a blast of something like rough dusk,
and a roar,
a windy, whooshing bellow of fire,
as children,

their faces illuminated and hot,
stare with mischievous awe
at the tree,
an instantaneous ball of thunderous flames.

And then my friends empty *their* pockets —
potatoes, halved, smeared with butter, wrapped in tin foil;
they toss them into the flames
where they are forgotten until much later,
when we'll skate off the ice,
tired and getting cold,
and to our delight,
remember those blackened, silver spheres
cratered and resting there among the fading embers,
ready to be unwrapped,
split open with our gloved hands,
salted, peppered, and eaten,
the best thing we've ever tasted,
our breath and the steam from the potatoes
rising around us,
little signals calling us to gather
much later,
under a cold blue sky
that won't exist for decades.

CONFESSION

Spring, 1967

It was very sad, he thought. The things men carried inside. The things men did or felt they had to do. – "The Things They Carried," Tim O'Brien

1

Fear overwhelmed me,
though it was cryptic,
weight covering the skin,
and when panic rose with unexpected velocity
I'd tear through the Yellow Pages,
look for a psychiatrist,
call the number,
and explain to the receptionist
that I was going to Viet Nam,
I was petrified,
losing my mind.

And the receptionist was always sweet and compassionate,
and would have me make an appointment,
which was not why I called.
I wanted immediate relief
right there on the phone,
but then the fear would subside,
and I'd never show up.

2

I'd play solitaire on my bed deep into night.
The rules were simple:
Win, don't die in Nam.

Lose. Die.
I'd play over and over until I won.
Then I'd change the rules.
You have to win two in a row not to die.

3

There was lots of screaming
in the halls of East Hartford High School.
I'd be nodding in some interminable class
when a primordial sob would kill my reverie.
And everyone knew what it meant.
Somebody's girlfriend torn down by the news —
another dead boy,
the kids in the class staring wide-eyed at each other.

And in the oppressive stillness
I'd feel the adrenaline,
which still shames me;
it felt good, that knowledge
of someone else's death.
It was a rush
in some reprehensible, degrading way,

And when I dreamed of being shot,
it was never painful or frightening in the soft
    framework of sleep.
What was upsetting only happened when I woke:
thoughts of leaving my girl for an *eternity*
paralyzed me,
but I was aware of the depth of my spinelessness,
and could not have cared less.

I'd pretend my dreams scared me,
talk about how I was afraid of death,
but it wasn't true.

What did I know about dying in a war?

And besides, my fear was more egotistical,
the juvenile, fostered fear
of leaving the safety
of the small things I thought I knew.

4

I never told Suzanne that I loved her.
She wasn't my girlfriend,
and Jimmy was my best friend.
Even after a sniper's round plowed through Jimmy's neck,
and he was KIA his third week in Nam,
I never said to Suzanne
Do you know that I love you?
although I did hug her as she wept,
and told her everything would be all right,
though what I was really thinking
was how exciting it was to be holding her
behind the Ten Pin Bowling Alley,
a brown paper bag skittering across the parking lot,
its mouth wide,
breathing in the filthy, drab air.

Later I drove in circles around Mammoth Mart,
trying to cry for my friend who was dead,
for his girlfriend who was shattered,
but I couldn't,
not about that.

What I did was cry for myself because I'd be leaving.
I didn't want to leave.
I wanted to stay in East Hartford
and have the war go away.
I was 18 years old,
pretending to know about love,
about war,
about the ways people die.

5

At Fort Dix one night
I cried in my rack,
but that wasn't real either.
They were forced tears,
and on July 4, 1967,
I made my two bunk mates
sit up consoling me,
though the only thing wrong was that
I wanted their attention.

I learned to Brass-O my belt buckle into a gold mirror,
spit-shine my boots until my index finger was a raisin,
and starch my uniform so it stood at attention waiting for me.
I memorized the book of General Orders
and shouted them into Lt. Pfiefer's face —
"Sir, my third General Order is
To report all violations of orders I am instructed to enforce, Sir!"
—not because I gave a damn about the General Orders
but because if I got named the Colonel's Orderly,
I could go home for 72 hours.

But when that happened
home was alien and sad

and my girlfriend and I either fought or made up
in the woods near North End Park,
weighed down by something
I couldn't put my finger on.

And at Dix there was James Clark,
who I helped beat because he never changed his underwear.
A bunch of guys had warned him
but he said he didn't care,
and so one night we threw him a blanket party
and I kicked as hard as I could,
even though I liked James very much,
and comforted him the very next day,
telling him that the guys who had done this
should be court-martialed,
and that I didn't give a good goddam
about his underwear.

6

On Wednesday nights the USO
would bus girls in from Camden
to dance with the troops,
and I'd meet Mary and we'd talk and kiss,
but Camden was farther away than Phnom Penh,
and there were no sad good-byes,
no promises to call or write;
there was only the subtle passing of fall,
the temperature dropping,
the days darkening,
and Mary eventually settling into the past,
a fragment of memory, tiny, enduring, and vague.

7

At Port Authority once
I was sitting on a bench
working on a crossword puzzle,
and waiting for a train,
when an old man wobbled stumbling out of a bathroom,
bloody and begging for help;

I glanced up from my puzzle for a moment,
then casually returned to 23 across,
telling myself something like
This happens all the time in New York.
No biggie.
Mind your business.

And coming home on a Greyhound bus one night,
I sat two seats behind the driver.
I could see the speedometer.
We were doing 110,
which shocked me.
I'll never forget.

I pretended to be asleep,
and the fat man next to me
also pretended to sleep, I think,
because he was leaning all his weight against me,
stroking my thigh,
and I let him.

8

Prior to '67, when things really heated up,
the National Guard and the Army Reserves
were the first choices for lots of guys.
Get into one of those
and it was no Nam for you.
Six months stateside, then home,
living the safe life,
denying the booby traps
and the sticky flames of napalm.
A meeting a month,
a party of weekend warriors.
Two weeks in the summer,
playing army during the day,
drinking all night.

But the Guard and the Reserves slammed shut.
That was it. Trapped.
No way out except Canada, jail,
or the labor-intensive C.O.

But I never went to Viet Nam.
The unconscionable blindness of Fortune intervened
in the person of Master Sergeant James Stanizzi,
my father's brother.

My father called in a blood favor,
and Master Sergeant Stanizzi infiltrated
the offices of the State Armory,
manipulated the file folders,
and the next morning I was on my way to Fort Dix,
a private in the "closed" Army National Guard.

And the collateral damage?

A boy my age, who would have been inducted
into the Guard next
was notified that, unfortunately, the Guard was full
and that he'd be on his way to the jungle.

At St. Mary's Elementary School they'd taught us
that Confession meant absolution and healing,
that after your penance,
after you'd made amends for your wrongdoings,
you'd feel a sense of perfect well-being and peace.

My penance has been to carry that boy
with me always,
carry that boy whose folder got moved,
that boy whose name I never knew,
carry him and keep him alive
for as long as I live.

HIGH AND INSIDE

That stuff I used to smoke
would render baseball new
and fascinating and notably odd.

No irrational stress about
who won or lost;
just those little guys on the TV,

dressed so strangely
in their tights and knee socks,
scurrying around willy-nilly,

scampering left and right,
waving clubs,
and throwing a ball around

against a backdrop
of high dazzling lights
and crowds of people.

The whole scene was
gloriously nonsensical.
I'd turn the sound off

and sit there smiling
with amused consternation
at this silly, complicated ordeal.

It was summer —
the blazing fastball of heat lightning,
the bat crack of thunder,

and me, clutching my knees to my chest,
alone in the hot night,
high and inside.

THE HAT

She had given me the hat as a peace offering
during one of our
learning to like one another
counseling sessions.

It was one of those paperboy hats,
brown plaid,
that looked good sitting catawampus
on my head.

I did everything in that hat,
and I was in such a good mood
that I even painted the yellowed kitchen ceiling
a nice soft white.

But the counseling didn't take,
and I slept on the living room floor for three years.
Along the way my hat vanished
and I thought about it all the time.

One day I needed to borrow something,
I don't recall what,
from the guy next door,
and to my amazement,

here he comes,
wearing *my* hat.
I was stunned and delighted.
Something that made sense.

"Man! That's where my hat went!" I said,
relieved of the obsession
of wondering what the hell
I had done with it.

But my neighbor was instantly belligerent.
"This is not your hat.
This is my hat.
This hat was a gift, man!"

For a moment I thought about straightening him out
but saw that it would be pointless,
so I walked away, keeping at bay something like
raging wounded liberation and massive silence,

never mentioning until now
the afternoon I found my hat,
that stubborn spot of white paint
still on the brim.

PROMISE

for Phil Bannock

Our friendship was crumbling
and held together with Black Velvet, herb,
and your '72 Valiant.

I'd plead with you not to drive like a lunatic,
and you, ever smooth,
assured me you wouldn't.

Then we'd drive nonchalantly
to the mouth of the Scantic River,
where we'd fish deep into the night,

and drink and smoke
until the night became a living thing,
and we would hide there, invisible.

Later we'd find our way
back to the Valiant
and fall in.

In and out of dreamy consciousness
I'd say
"How fast we going?"

ZZ Top thumped over the static
and the snarl
of the hole in the muffler.

"Hundred an' ten," you'd say calmly,
"One. Hundred. And fuckin' ten."
And the hot wind of late July

slapped me around a little in the passenger seat
until the trees were crazed creatures
and I'd whisper to myself,

Hell yeah,
leaning back in peace,
the world roaring into me.

NORRIE

1

The apartment we shared
during our divorces
was a definite upgrade
from you hiding with your tears
behind the couch in the game room at Aetna,
or me driving the length
of Old Main Street every night,
nursing a fifth of Black Velvet.

We were hoarders,
and we stuffed the apartment
with the debris of our previous lives,
saving it from the curb,
that junk that was ours alone
before the vows, the kids, the demolition.

2

Empty jars of salsa,
torn Tostitos bags
and a smell that nearly
turned me away every time,
but there was nowhere else to go.

You had Norrie, an indoor cat,
skittery and black,
who stayed out of sight,
hiding in the layers of trash,

coming out nervously to nibble
on the blocks of cheese
we'd toss on the floor,

and in the clearing
in the center of the dining room,
where you'd hung a punching bag,
the two of us took turns
beating holy hell
out of everything that was.

3

You left for a weekend once during a heat wave —
95 plus for days.

In the middle of the night,
naked in front of the fan,
dripping sweat,
I roared to myself
that this was the right thing.
Norrie was in heat
and howling a primal, plaintive demand
to be set free.

I tried to comfort her
by picking her up
but there was nothing there that was not wild,
and she attacked,

all claws and teeth,
and raked my naked body
from neck to navel.

I threw her across the rubble
and wailed,
as ribbons of blood
emerged on my chest.

Norrie cowered across the room,
all hisses and growls,
and out of the hot night,
neighborhood toms flung themselves
again and again
against the screens,
screaming to be let in,
while Norrie and I,
stupefied,
could see no way out.

CELEBRITIES WITH EGG ROLLS

What are these,
So withered, and so wild in their attire,
That look not like th' inhabitants o' th' earth
And yet are on' t? – *Macbeth,* Act I, Sc. 3

In the red vinyl booth
in the poorly lit food court
behind the escalator
in the casino,
a tiny, skeletal woman with Auden's face
and Jane Mansfield's hair
sits motionless,
grinning at some far-away funny business.

Beside her,
shoulder to shoulder,
a mouse-faced man chews on a golf pencil
and pours over a racing form.
He never looks up,
not even when his choppy fingers
ratchet forward,
clasp the coffee cup,
and find his mouth.

The third person in the booth
has found Johnny Cash's clothes
rolled in a ball somewhere,
and his mutton chops,
spray painted black,
need a trim.
He ignores the other two

who ignore him.
He's fretfully surveying the food court —
looking for Peter Lorre?
The whole scene, including me,
is reflected in his post-cataract sunglasses.
I am assuming that David Lynch
has stepped to the men's room for a moment.

Ms. Auden picks up an egg roll,
shiny and heavy and huge,
and brings it shakily to her skinny lips
as the lights in the food court flicker once.
The mouse-faced man looks
over the top of his glasses
and Johnny's head twitches once,
nearly imperceptibly.

I've come here to eat cheap
and wait for things to settle down,
and now it's time to make my move.
It's well past dawn.
I've lost everything and then some.
The machines must be heating up by now,
the casino barren as Araby.

IS IS

The thing, the way we look directly at
each other, speak that line, the qualifier, alibi,
stumble-john of a funky, lame excuse
improvised with hardly any thought
beyond the fact that we're not going to play,
flimsy line as solid as a stone
yet transparent, a feeble little tale,
emergency exit lie of necessity
that we've all used in love or otherwise
to squirm away from something genuine
because, well the thing is is that
there is a fiction we must attend,
a fabrication we simply cannot miss.

FICTION

*"... to advance to the muzzles of guns with
perfect nonchalance!"*   –Walt Whitman

I want to get all my mistakes,
injustices, and regrets,
real or imagined,
and trick them into thinking
that they've gotten the better of me,
that I'm finally dispatched.

I want them all to meet
in some remote location,
like maybe a big house in the country,
where they'll sit by a stone fireplace,
drinking Courvoisier
and smoking La Gloria Cubanos,
laughing at how they used me,
made a fool of me.
I want them to feel absolutely certain
that I'm gone.

What they won't know
is that I'll be outside hiding in the woods,
camo on, face blacked,
getting their bodyguards lined up
in my cross-hairs.
They won't hear the shots
over their loud boasting.

Then I'll appear,
to their terrified surprise,

ghostly behind the couch,
and they'll beg me to reconsider,
yelling, "Wait! There's been a mistake!"
But it will be too late.
I'll take them out one at a time.

Then I'll mess with a gas pipe
that just happens to run down the wall
right near the fireplace.
I'll pop it with the butt end of my automatic
and it'll start to hiss,
my cue to saunter out indifferently,
rifle slung over my shoulder.

I'll open the front door
and walk slowly across the lawn
into the foggy night,
perfect nonchalance,
as behind me the big house
explodes in a series of deafening volcanic eruptions,
boiling flames a hundred feet high,
sending shards of wood and metal and embers
raining down on everything,
explosion after explosion,
but I will not flinch.

Metallica's *Fight Fire With Fire*
will have started to play in the background
as I stroll in silhouette against the monstrous blaze,
all the consequences of my every indiscretion
dissolving in smoke and flames
as I disappear into the fog,
clutching a secret no one will ever know
but you and me.

MOWING THE APPLES

In the fall,
as an excuse to have a cigar,
mow the lawn every other day,
oil-thirsty tappets knocking out a racket
all over the neighborhood,
vague smoke-scent of tobacco and oil;
cultivate the cigar ash until it drops on the belly,
then toss the stub onto the lawn,
forgetting before it lands where it falls —
and later,
quite unintentionally,
mow over it,
spewing old wet tobacco
and the surprise
of Grandpa's pungent sour breath,
then mow the apples,
run over the past again,
and cleanse the palate with sweeter memories.

KAYAK

for my son Jason and my grandson Jonah

The rainiest June since 1989,
and the weighty vault of gray clouds
spills open every day —
three inches yesterday!
Enormous trees lie down in wet grass
as easy as jewelweed uprooted
and let the rain bathe over them,
their ragged crowns of roots exposed,
as in the peripheral hills
lightning shorts out the sky
and bottom-heavy thunder
snarls in the distance,
looking for attention.
But my son calls anyway,
eager to defy the persistent weather,
wanting to scull the kayak
through the day's foggy midday funk,
the mist parting to reveal the sun
and us emerging from the haze.

So I agree to go,
though I'm not in the mood.
The weather sucks,
but we climb into the tandem kayak anyway,
my grandson, my son, and me.
The air is sodden and thick,
and the gray sky so low I can touch it.

We seat ourselves in the boat,
triplets, matryoshka dolls —
Jonah in front,
the smallest,
the one everyone wants to hold,
curious and smooth,
hand over the side,
parting the water with his fingers,
searching for everything
that lies between and beneath.

His father, Jason, is in the middle,
nicked up,
largely overlooked,
and huddled between infancy and old age,
his past a kind of love.

And me in the stern,
grandfather, father.
still large enough to hold them both,
but worn by light,
worn by darkness,
and growing tired
of the long, silent stories
of men who, once they go,
can never return.

VOICES

What took me
completely by surprise
was that it was me:
my voice, in my mouth.

"In the Waiting Room," Elizabeth Bishop

There are times when, in my mother's voice,
her father's voice distracts me from her words,
doppelganger-speak in some translation
that sounds as if she's simply saying *Hi* —
when in truth it is her father come to say,
in language of the living, that he'd like
for me to take a moment and to think
of all the time we spent in shady joints,
our elbows on a sticky wooden bar,
the half-light and acrid smell of booze,
stale beer and the years-old reek of smoke.

I also hear it when my daughter speaks —
my mother's voice addressing me as *Dad?*
asking me if I can watch the kids,
and when I answer, my aunt, my mother's sister,
answers back, but with her father's voice
in which I hear the tinny timbre of
his eccentric mother, Grandma Far-Away,
asking if I'd like some "funny water"
in a voice my other daughter borrows
to bring me up to speed on all her plans,
sounding just like Uncle Rocky did
when he'd grin a menacing grin and talk

about his tennis game or bothering girls
in the flickering darkness of the theater.

Then my boy speaks with his brother's voice,
but it's my father, calling to say his wife
is going to have a child, their first. We share
the joy with jokes of our advancing age
and hopes that it will be a boy to keep
our name alive. I smile and clear my throat,
but it's my father's throat, my father's cough,
and there we are, the living and the dead,
the living carrying on as best we can,
the dead alive in everything we say.

TRUMPET VINE

for Jason and Jessica and Jonah

It's not the notes you play, it's the notes you don't play.

– Miles Davis

In 1951 my great-grandmother
gave my mother a piece
of the trumpet vine
that bullied the border of white pines
around her West Hartford yard
which was always deeply shaded,
damp and cool,
and in 1990 my mother
gave me a sprig from that same vine;
it had taken over her woven wire fence,
and even ran out along the lawn,
little rivulets of neap tide vines.

We waited ten years
for a sign of orange trumpets,
but the vine only grew green,
higher, fuller, silent,
its stem thickening,
its web of tendrils closing slowly
around the deck post and up 25 feet,
each frond a spray of jagged leaves,
the new ones rusty and small,
sweet and impatient reaching up,
the old ones nodding heavily toward the ground.

Last summer I gave you a cutting,
and this April there it was,
a little green curl of hope,
and I thought of my great-grandmother
planting that vine a hundred or so years ago,
and wondered where she had gotten it:
had the rabbi next door given her a twig,
complaining that it had taken over his garage,
or had she brought a piece back from a Cape Cod marsh,
thinking it would look pretty beneath her trees,
never dreaming of its copiousness,
or was it already in her yard when she moved in,
something that became hers alone
yet was abundant enough to be given away freely?

These days our vine is crowded with trumpets
sounding their silent articulations
in praise of the muted past
and looking into the propitious future,
and even the thunder that tries
to play above the trumpets
is drowned out by the hush.

III. AFTER ELLIS ISLAND

PROMISES AFTER ELLIS ISLAND

Your names separate
from English sentences
and knock against the teeth,
small pits of words, hard as stone
and always what they always were,
despite the promises that must have
echoed off the high ceilings
in the The Great Hall.

Tsue Pap is moving to yet another apartment
because they raised the rent;
he is frantic in the dirt cellar,
digging hole after hole,
looking for the money he buried one night,
drunk on Guinea Red.

Jit Ate is rocking and chanting,
waving the framed picture
of a young soldier,
telling and retelling the story
of her handsome Johnny Boy,
who never came home from the war.

Jah Doze, frying medallions of chicken blood
in a tiny cast iron frying pan,
is tightening the rag around her shattered right wrist,
pulling the rag with her teeth and her left hand,
the tattered bracelet squeezing
the break she could never afford to fix.

Zeta Zeen, the sexy one,
is flouncing across Albany Avenue,
pocketbook locked at her elbow,
stocking seams nose-diving
down the backs of her legs
and into red second-hand stiletto heels.

And *Sdunny Ale,* pragmatic and kind,
is peeling an exotic banana for the very first time,
gnawing the bitter yellow skin
and tossing aside the long white pit,
deceptively soft
and as easy to choke on as disillusion.

COMET

Not until years later did I wonder if,
as you stood naked at the bathroom mirror,
you were examining the thick crescent
ripped from your armpit all the way to where
your breast had been,
or if, in the silky blue of your eyes,
you caught a glimpse of yourself as a girl
and were you thinking of your husband
when you ran a finger across the bone under your eye.

Watching you get ready for bed,
I'd marvel at your hair, which was always up
in a tight, flat, white bun
against the back of your head,
until it was time for you to brush it,
and then you'd let it tumble down your back,
white and shining from the top of your head
down to your knees, white,
and then eight inches of jet black at the end,
a comet dropping headlong into the past.

WATCHES

Augustino says, "For knock-off Rolexes
I'll drive to Arthur Avenue
like I'm drivin' down the street
to fuckin' 7-Eleven for a coffee.
Fifteen bucks a watch
and you can't tell
unless you look at the second hand.
The Rolex sweeps.
These tick.
Who gives a fuck.
And besides, it's nice to have
a little somethin' in the trunk
to make a couple extra dollars.
What do you care?
Three grand. Fifteen bucks.
When somebody asks you
what time is it
it's still ten of fuckin' nine
on both of 'em
and when the train flies by
going 90 miles an hour
your gold watch flashing in the window
it ain't nobody gonna know
the fuckin' difference."

LYE

for my grandmother, Teresa Cirone DeFeo

It got around the neighborhood
that Mr. Gloss had drunk lye.
His daughter found him dead on the cellar stairs;
he had gotten caught having an affair,
and although I was only 11,
I had a pretty good idea what that meant.
My real confusion had to do with lye;
I had no idea what it was,
though I do recall that the idea of Mr. Gloss
dead on the stairs was fascinating.

Little by little,
through overheard fragments,
I began to comprehend,
and with that understanding came disbelief.
Of all the ways you might choose to go out,
why would you would choose to drink lye?
Did it have something to do with a desire
to destroy the tongue that had deceived the spouse,
that had whispered the first suggestion of betrayal
and entered the mouth of the other woman?

I thought of what it must have felt like,
that smoldering lye,
that bitter burning lye erasing the lies that filled his mouth,
all that seething deception and love, desire and confusion
boiling up inside until it finally undid reason.

And years later
on a snowy gray afternoon in February,
I was driving you home.
You were small and cold
and when I asked about my great-grandfather,
your father, your silence became palpable,
filled the car,
and then your tears came.

He had a girlfriend,
his *goomah,*
you said,
and this had shattered your gentle mother,
and I was stunned by disbelief.

How could this be?
Mr. Gloss, in East Hartford, Connecticut,
and in Italy, your delicate mother in Provincia de Potenza,
the two of them wounded by the same lie,
Mr. Gloss on the planks of his cellar stairs,
and your mother on the dirt floor in her kitchen,
an empty bottle of lye on the wooden table,
while outside somewhere
a man is always whispering into a phone,
a woman is always starting a cold car on a winter night,
and in a little motel room
a small lamp washes the knotty pine walls
a hazy, melancholy yellow.

COMMUNION

When the avenue was cleaned
by whirlybirds of seeds
in a polished city with sparkling windows,
I'd sit in a bucket full of water on hot September days,
or lie on the cool linoleum floor between
my grandmother's big brown shoes
and stare up into the mystery
of snaps and nylon under her dress.
She was an excommunicant,
and Tony the nice man with a wife and children
would be there most days,
sitting at the sunny table and speaking
so softly I couldn't hear.

My grandfather was gone by then,
and his red-headed daughter put on a bus to somewhere
by her red-headed mother Jenny the prostitute,
and whenever my grandfather did come around
he'd always wipe the corners of his eyes
with the backs of his wrists
while he talked to me.

The only thing my grandmother ever needed
she couldn't have,
until the day at Mass
when I drank the Blood of Christ,
kept it wet on my lips
and took His body cupped in my hands,
back to her in the pew
where I nudged her,

opened my hands to the great disobedience,
and nodded.

"No," she said as I kissed her mouth,
Blood of Christ,
broke His body,
ate half,
put the other to her mouth,
Body of Christ,
salvation's relief shining through
the guilt in her face.

FIRE MAN

for Derek Gaston

The fire pit was a rusty fifty-five gallon drum
buried in the yard. It was filled with sand
nearly to the top, with hunks of split
wood and crumpled newspaper neatly ordered.
Derek struck a match and held it to a corner
of the paper; it caught slowly, a tiny flame

pulsing and dancing to a larger flame.
He played his thigh like a conga drum,
took the bottle of Patron, drained the corner,
and with his heel drew a big "D" in the sand.
His working life was disciplined and ordered,
but away from things ablaze it had been split

and charred to an ember. The moon split
wide open, igniting his face in flames.
He spoke of the night he tried to set his life in order,
walking into the blazing sunset, the drum
of the moon rising, his thoughts like sand.
He lit a cigarette, blew smoke from the corner

of his mouth, and recalled how cornered
he had felt. Sparks and fire and smoke split
the summer sky as he poked the sand
in the pit and rearranged the wood, flames
and cinders in a chaos of fire, the old drum
hot now, and Derek's face an order

of unearthly manic joy as he spoke of the order
of things — "Don't let fire get you cornered.
Most powerful force on earth. The drumming
thunder of blistering heat and smoke will split
an entire forest, and burn your memory with flames."
He dragged his sneaker across the hot sand

where the *D* was, erased it from the sand,
and smiled at some thought. "A log," he ordered,
the joy illuminating his face, wild flames
smoldering in his eyes. No longer cornered,
he picked up a fiery log with his hand and split
the darkness with that torch, a burning drum-

stick he cornered us with, shadows on the sand.
Thunder drummed night senseless, and order
fell down around him in flames, burning and split.

BROKEN

for my son Jason

The young man's bruises have the luster of metal,
and he weeps whenever there is talk
of winding roads which shine with the danger of rain,
roads bordered by blackened trees which throw

down their heavy shadows thick and wet;
and he stares off into a world that you,
from the comfort of your tenuous routines,
can not imagine, though you certainly try —

what else can he do in the presence of such
an intimate struggle but try to ignore the sun
that could deceive him into believing that all
he has to do is walk out through the light

that heats the windows of his sunny room,
that fills the room, as summer does, with thoughts
of children's faces streaked with sweat from play,
that all he has to do is start his car,

and drive with certainty into the crowd
that races blindly through the countryside,
driven by the fatal misconception
that everything will always be all right.

SON

for my son Jonathan

The facile breeze weaves its way between
the lashes of your eyes as you stare out
across the lights of summer…the fireflies,
the silent moon, the quietude of the stars,

the prison lights clustered in the valley
like a crowded, earthbound constellation,
the occasional headlights of a traveling car,
the tower that blinks against the black horizon.

And you stare out in search of an opening,
a small and quiet place where you might go,
a space in which the sun and moon will rise,
and one of those you love will not be there

to bruise that sky or kill that light with anger,
and no one speaks, not even in a whisper.

TIRELESS NEIGHBOR

Good fences make good neighbors.

"Mending Wall," Robert Frost

Someone had stolen
all four of my tires
and I found my car sitting there
on the bare rims.

I tried frantically to call
the tow-truck guy
who would come and fix the problem
but I couldn't find his number
on my cell phone.

Then, as is the way in dreams,
things suddenly seemed normal.
I was driving along just fine,
no worries,
cruising somewhere,
until I became aware of
scraping metal,
remembered the tires were gone,
pulled over in a storm of sparks,
and resumed the desperate, futile search
for the tow-truck guy's number.

Driven by the knowledge
that I was late for something,
I repeated this scene over and over —
pulling into a 7-Eleven,

a school,
a police station.

Then I was awake and stumbling
into the bathroom,
recalling vaguely
that the lunatic neighbor across the street
had her car up on blocks all week, tireless.

This is the neighbor who complained
that my white picket fence
was exactly like hers,
who rooted through my trash
to see how much I drank,
who said "I don't say *Merry Christmas*
to people like you,"
while she stood ringing
the Salvation Army bell
in front of CVS.
Now she was marauding my dreams,
stealing my hypnopompic tires.

When I fell asleep again
my tires were still gone,
and there she was,
lumbering around a foggy corner,
lug wrench in hand,
the sun struggling to rise
behind her.

APPLE TORTURE

"Mrs. Walter, can we go to the apple torture?"
A question from one of Diane Walter's kindergarteners

He must realize that what he will see
at the apple torture
will be a grove of trees,
their branches arched
and exhausted with full apples,
and that it will be nothing like, say,
going to the hanging,
though both have their obvious similarities.

And he could not possibly imagine
that his question would bring to mind
the crowds that gathered
for the pressing,
speculating which of the heavy stones
would be used next,
and would it be the one.

And my guess is
that he would be frightened by the notion
of attending the stoning
where he might actually be expected to participate,
though my sad hunch is that, eventually,
he'd warm to the idea.

Going to the crucifixion
might be more relaxing;
he could saunter up the hill
with his peanut butter and jelly sandwich,

a couple of juice boxes,
an apple,
have a seat with the rest of the gang.

I imagine he'd be mesmerized by all of them:
the drowning, the dragging,
the strappado, the garotte,
the water boarding,
the hurling from a great height,
and the ever-intriguing
being tied in a sack with feral cats.
He is in kindergarten, after all.

No. For now I say leave it as it is.
It's not such a bad thing
that this kid thinks that
going to the torture
means a day out of school,
a ride on the thumpy yellow bus
with his friends and his teacher whom he loves,
and being deposited in a throng of fragrant trees

and standing in the cool shade
polishing a big apple on his shirt,
the only rumble the tumble of the cider mill,
the only discomfort
the bend of branches abundant with fruit,
an ache that is relieved by simply reaching up,
plucking off an apple,
and standing in the momentary faith of childhood
filled with the marvel
of having gone to the apple torture.

FIREFLY

for my grandson Michael

In the heaviness
of a July evening,
I watch a parade
of my grandchildren
following the quirky
lilt of a firefly.
Michael leads,
arms outstretched,
a plastic cup in one hand,
hope in the other.
It's slow work
and silent,
pursuing that little
blossom of light
all over the yard.

Right in front of him,
between cup and palm,
it vanishes into darkness
and catches fire again
just out of reach over his head,
and I feel utterly
his urge to capture
that tiny bolt of light,
the thrill of not knowing
when it will vanish,
where it will reappear,
and will he ever

hold it for a moment up close
to marvel at the tiny creature
that finds its way
just as Michael does,
guided by the light
of its own little body.

IV. MORE THAN ENOUGH

FAWN

A depilated dog would not look well.
Dress up! Dress up and dance at Carnival!

    "The Pink Dog," Elizabeth Bishop

In the carnival of lights and shadows at dawn,
a small bony dog stands in the road,
Elizabeth's dog, watching me curiously
from the center line, so I slow for her,
and then I see the dabs of softened white.
Her right ear twitches a wary cautious twitch,
and she lopes into the woods, leaving me with
a sense of joy at seeing this tiny fawn.
But just as I am about to leave, I hear
her squawk, and see her just behind the scrub
at the side of the road, where she is watching me,
her wise and fearful eyes too big for her.
What are you doing, I say, and where is your mother?
She hears my voice, and steps back to the road;
looking me straight in the eyes, she bleats a question,
but before I can respond, another car
comes speeding by and off she runs for good,
before I even have the chance to say
that I would lie down near her in the woods
while she slept, sheltered on a nest of leaves,
and when her mother returned, then I would go,
having kept her safe from the likes of me.

HAWK

I only saw it once,
though *saw* is an exaggeration.
It was something less than a glimpse,
some insignificant wisp of a passing idea
at the far end of my peripheral vision,
the blurred silhouette of a hawk
carrying in its talons
the blurred silhouette of a bird.

This was after I had found
the first feathers,
a catbird's,
and then, twice, blue jays'
feathers arranged neatly on the ground
in the shape of a starfish
or a God's Eye.

That was all:
no plucked, hollow-boned body,
no blood.
Just a composition of feathers
there on the grass
beneath the feeders,
a talking circle,
the ritual of *What is left unsaid,*
the hawk lifting
the plucked and keening body
and perhaps the talking feather too,
leaving the rest behind,

as if the hawk's ascension
were affirmation that
when you are carried away
you must shed everything,
what you have said,
what it was you meant to say,
and, yes, even your
lovely, momentary feathers.

MICE

I hear them in the walls
after night's dark heart starts beating
and snow's enormous silence
finally settles down in moonlight.
From their nests
of soup labels and candle wax,
thread and onion skins,
they open their small eyes;
silence has touched them
to say night has come,
it's safe now,
and the tiny, voracious mechanism
of their hunger
turns away from nothing
in the furrows of their dusky world.
They even eat the sweet, soft glue
that binds my books,
and later the pages themselves,
whole chapters,
while I dream that they've nibbled
the soft edges of sleep
and entered in droves,
thousands of them
pouring through the holes they've made,
laughing and running upright on their hind legs,
bigger than me,
speaking in tongues a language I understand,
showing me how they do it,
spreading their wings
and flying straight up out of sight.

SNAKES

It's August and I haven't touched the kayak
since early June when I couldn't leave it alone;
the school year over, summer had begun,
the river up and stocked, the days becoming
warmer and longer. The process of unwinding
was now my job, and every day I worked
to get it right, drifting on the copper
colored river that slowed and grew more shallow
every day. But soon my focus changed,
and I moved on to chores around the house:
unclog the gutter, clean the cellar out,
re-cement the crumbling steps in front.
And before too long the goldenrod appeared
and Sweet Joe Pye was roughing up the wetland.

When I finally flipped the kayak to wash it out,
there you were, the wriggling two of you,
moving in every direction away at once,
nothing like the evil symbolism,
temptation manifest, that we were taught.
You were more like lovers I'd disturbed,
who couldn't vanish fast enough into
the shade of the weltered bittersweet that grew
up and through the ash tree by the pond,
and so I stood in the wake of your hasty departure
as you rippled off, less like Caril and Charles,
Fred and Rosemary, or even Bonnie and Clyde,
and more like Lancelot and Guinevere,
or Adam and Eve running away from fear
before something happened they could not change.

TREEFROG

Though there were no trees near me at all,
you were right there,
inhabiting a hot sheet of billowing night air,
your glass song sporadic and sure,
an unambiguous sketch of the very sound you intended,
a replicated warble whose source I needed to find,
to see, without comprehending of course,
the mechanics of that primal chime,
so I lay belly down on the deck
and tried to be still and listen.
I was shocked to a start by your appearance;
you were motionless enough to be imaginary,
black eyes in a small gray lump stiller than stone
there in the pool's blue light at the water's edge,
and with your mouth closed,
the bagpipe of your throat filled,
your whole body vibrated,
and little veins, tattoos of tiny rivers,
flowed on the globe of your throat,
as you repeated the same simple song
over and over again,
so perfect that its sameness was its beauty,
and *that is more than enough,*
I said to myself,
that is more than enough,
more than enough.

FRONT

Disastrous drought they're calling it,
nothing more than a trace of rain in two months,
but yesterday's rumor of showers crackled
over radios and televisions,
and in anticipation, the ordering of things began:
gather up the stray tools, put the tractor away,
tell the geraniums that soon, soon it will be all right,
and go to bed with one ear open, listening
for the sympathetic whisper of rain in the trees,
and the silent sigh of the landscape
and everything hidden there.

Now the pacific hiss of morning rain,
sun held down under clouds and fog,
and the rooms of the house soften with dusky shadows.
May it rain all day long and never brighten,
not even for a moment.
And may the plants lift their faces,
streaked with dusty rain water,
and like children running around the yard,
catch the drops in their open, smiling mouths.

THE LANGUAGE OF TREES

If the trees speak in the forest
and no one is there
is the language of the trees audible,
or do the words drip from the leaves
down the rough lengths of their bodies
and seep into the ground,
the roots,
and is that language then
as simple as holding hands in the dark,
never speaking a single word?

WAITING

Back to the shore where the ocean strokes the rocks.
The hunkered barnacles are small volcanoes,
and the slow, soft turns of the periwinkles
hold them fast against the great blue dream

of the sea from which the glistening terns emerge,
shades of shooting stars that tumble up
out of the rocking wetness of the sky
where candy-colored boats bob in the swells

and people wave, their faces made of glass.
This is the time when all of our desires
have been diminished to the simple hum
of wind across the fishing line, and sun

exploding from a cloudlessness that heats
the beads of sweat that glitter on your chest.

PATH

In the early hours of morning when darkness drains
out of the sky and into the tops of trees
whose silhouettes undulate through the rising fog —
early morning, crawling from the well of night,

your fears still hanging off you like old rags,
you hear the grunt of frogs around the pond,
a lexicon of confidence and life,
and you hear the mockingbird, who you are sure

must listen carefully despite his zeal,
and deep in the hills the Montrealer sounds
its throaty note and fills you full of thoughts
of other worlds, of sounds within a dream,

and distant birds fleck the panorama
with what they have to sing, and you are drawn
through this early mist down to the pond,
along these muddy halls where spider webs

cling to your face and arms with delicate tension,
a gentle hint of restraint that wraps you up
and slows you down and stuns you into life.

ABOUT THE AUTHOR

John L. Stanizzi has delighted readers and listeners throughout New England and (thanks in part to his presence on Garrison Keillor's *Writer's Almanac*) beyond the Northeast. He is the author of *Ecstasy Among Ghosts,* now in its fourth printing, *Sleepwalking,* and *Windows.* His work has appeared in *The New York Quarterly, Tar River Poetry, Rattle, Freshwater, Passages North, The Spoon River Quarterly, Poet Lore, The Connecticut River Review,* and many other publications. Twice nominated for a Pushcart Prize, in 1998 Stanizzi was named New England Poet of the Year by The New England Association of Teachers of English. He has read at many venues throughout Connecticut, including RJ Julia Booksellers and the Arts Café Mystic (with Gerald Stern). In 2011 he introduced Dick Allen, Connecticut's Poet Laureate, at the Sunken Garden Poetry Festival, presenting a lecture and discussion session before the reading. In 2012 he presented a second Sunken Garden lecture, this time on Natasha Trethewey, Pulitzer Prize winner and newly-named U.S. Poet Laureate. He has judged the Connecticut Poetry Out Loud competition and the 2011 Connecticut Book Award for Poetry. John L. Stanizzi teaches English at Manchester Community College and Bacon Academy, where he also directed the theater program for fifteen years. He lives with his wife, Carol, in Coventry, Connecticut.

This book is set in Garamond Premier Pro, which had its genesis in 1988 when type-designer Robert Slimbach visited the Plantin-Moretus Museum in Antwerp, Belgium, to study its collection of Claude Garamond's metal punches and typefaces. During the mid-fifteen hundreds, Garamond—a Parisian punch-cutter—produced a refined array of book types that combined an unprecedented degree of balance and elegance, for centuries standing as the pinnacle of beauty and practicality in type-founding. Slimbach has created an entirely new interpretation based on Garamond's designs and on comparable italics cut by Robert Granjon, Garamond's contemporary.

To order additional copies of this book
or other Antrim House titles, contact the publisher at

Antrim House
21 Goodrich Rd., Simsbury, CT 06070
860.217.0023, AntrimHouse@comcast.net
or the house website (www.AntrimHouseBooks.com).

•

On the house website
in addition to information on books
you will find sample poems, upcoming events,
and a "seminar room" featuring supplemental biography,
notes, images, poems, reviews, and
writing suggestions.